Japanese fabric
flowers

SEARCH PRESS

Acknowledgements

The Publisher and author would like to extend their warm thanks to Clover for providing
all the flower and yo-yo makers used in this book.
www.clover-usa.com/en
Clover® products are available from sewing, craft and quilting stores.

Thank you to **La droguerie** for the accessories, the findings and most of the fabric:
http://www.ladroguerie.com

Dedication:
To Brigitte, Nadia and Stéphanie,
you are always in my thoughts.

First published in Great Britain in 2015
by Search Press Limited, Wellwood,
North Farm Road, Tunbridge Wells, Kent TN2 3DR

Reprinted 2016, 2017, 2019, 2020, 2021, 2022

First published by Fleurus Éditions, Paris, France
Original French title *Fleurs Kanzashi en Tissu*

Copyright © 2014 Fleurus Éditions
15/27, rue Moussorgski - 75895 Paris Cedex 18

Translation by Burravoe Translation Services

Typesetting by Greengate Publishing Services,
Tonbridge, Kent

Photography : Thierry Antablian
Contribution to photography : Sylvie Blondeau
Illustrations : Laurent Stefano

ISBN: 978-1-78221-228-7

Sylvie Blondeau

Japanese fabric flowers

65 decorative kanzashi flowers to make

Contents

Projects 26

Introduction

What is kanzashi?

The Japanese word *kanzashi* originally referred to the decorative pins that women used in their traditional hairstyles – skilful and precise works of art. They held in place elaborate floral arrangements made of natural or silk flowers.

By extension, fabric flowers made in the traditional Japanese style have adopted the kanzashi name. Whether as accessories on clothing, brooches or jewellery, decorations around the house or special-occasion table adornments, they are always a delight to the eye.

A simple technique

Kanzashi flowers are so easy and fun to make that you will soon be making them for every occasion. Children can join in too. All you need are a few small pieces of fabric, scissors, a needle and thread plus a dab of adhesive: an easy recipe for success. The most difficult task is deciding on colours and patterns.

Choice of fabrics

These flowers can be made with most fabrics, but the stiffness and thickness of the fabric will have a significant impact on the finished loo so choose with care:

Stiffer fabrics, such as linen or heavy silk, will allow you to make more structured flowers, but on the whole, it is best not to go too stiff: upholstery fabrics can often be too thick. A mini yo-yo (see page 22) made with thick material will tend to form a button shape rather than staying flat, which can be very pretty for the heart of a flower.

Medium-weight fabrics, such as dressmaking fabrics, are perfect for most of the flowers. Raw silk and cotton poplin are ideal and easy to work with.

Thin, light fabric makes it easier to form the gathers on small flowers, produce petals made up of multiple layers. They will also give you nice open flower heads on the bigger models. Avoid fabric that is too limp or which frays easily because the finishing will be more difficult.

Patterned fabric works just as well as plain fabric and there is no limit pattern size. In fact, fabrics with a big pattern offer different areas of colour that allow you to make flowers with variegated petals. With a bit of practice, you can enjoy yourself at the petal-folding stage, selecting the parts of the pattern that you want to show.

Where to start

Begin by making the basic flowers on pages 10–23, ideally using a selection of different fabrics to get a feel for what works best. In additio to the fabric for the petals you need a little felt for the backing and a button or bead for the flower centre. For each of the large projects the fabrics and findings required are provided in full.

Tools and materials

You won't need much to make your first kanzashi flower but once you have mastered the technique you can try more ambitious projects using layers of petals, adding costume jewellery findings to give the flowers more glamour or making simple projects specifically to show off your flowers.

Templates

The petals for many of the flowers start out as fabric circles or squares. To speed up the process, make templates first by tracing the shapes on to thin cardboard or template plastic. Use a ruler and set square or a compass to help you get accurate shapes.

Some flowers can only be made using a kanzashi flower maker, which are inexpensive and widely available. The most widely available are Clover® flower makers – they come in various shapes and sizes, as shown on pages 20–21.

Thread

Use a strong thread that matches your fabric to gather the petals and assemble the flowers.

Needle

You will need a long, thin needle to make the gathers on the petals. If the fabric is thick, you can always use a thimble to help you push the needle through.

Pins

Pins will help you to keep the petals folded before sewing. Alternatively, you can use clips.

Scissors

A small pair of sharp scissors is ideal for cutting out the fabric and snipping threads. Use a separate pair of scissors for cutting out the cardboard templates – if you use your scissors to cut anything but fabric, you may blunt them.

Glue

Use a sparing amount of textile adhesive to fix the petals to the felt base. For some projects you will also need multi-purpose glue to fix findings in place.

Felt

Each flower is stuck to a felt base, which neatens the back. Preferably, you should match the colour of the felt to the petals. You only need a small amount for each flower.

Synthetic stuffing

Use this to stuff the fabric pumpkins and pearls (see pages 22–23). This is widely available and often sold as toy stuffing or polyester stuffing. You could even buy a cheap pillow and use the stuffing from that.

Buttons

These are used to finish the centre of the flowers. Choose a button large enough to completely cover the hole in the middle of the petal. You can use ordinary sew-through or shank buttons, or self-cover buttons with the fabric of your choice. You can also use old, recycled buttons, preferably the ones with a shank on the back for attachment. Other accessories such as beads or costume jewellery findings can be used instead of buttons (see pages 24–25).

Simple kanzashi flowers

Instructions for making all these simple but beautiful flowers are given on the following pages. Think of them as training projects. Once you are familiar with these techniques, it's simply a matter of playing around with fabrics, shapes and sizes to make more advanced flowers.

Rosette, page 23

Flower 12, page 20

Flower 6, page 16

Pearl, page 22

Flower 3, page 14

Flower 7, page 17

Flower 1, page 12

Flower 10, page 19

Flower 9, page 18

Yo-yo, page 22

Flower 11, page 19

Rosette, page 23

Pearl, page 22

Flower 2, page 13

Pearl, page 22

Flower 5, page 15

Flower 16, page 20

Flower 14, page 20

Flower 8, page 17

Flower 15, page 20

Yo-yo, page 22

Pearl, page 22

Flower 13, page 20

Pumpkin, page 22

Flower 4, page 15

11

Flower 1

This flower has round, well-formed
petals and is very quick and easy
to make.

Materials: five circles of fabric 7.5cm (3in) in diameter, one felt circle
4cm (1½in) in diameter and one button at least 3cm (1¼in) in diameter
Size of finished flower: about 8cm (3¼in) in diameter

1 Fold each circle of fabric in half. Use your nail to press the fold. If the
fabric has a right and wrong side, make sure you fold it wrong
sides together.

2 Thread a needle with about 40cm (16in) of doubled thread. Tie a knot
in the end. Starting 5mm (¼in) from the edge, bring the needle up
through the first petal, leaving around 5cm (2in) of the knotted end
sticking out. Sew running stitches spaced around 2mm (⅛in) apart all
round the curved edge. Finish with the needle and thread underneath,
as shown.

3 With the same thread, continue in the same way along the curved
edge of each of the four remaining petals, always starting and finishing
underneath the petal. Pull the thread to gather the petals.

4 Knot the two ends of thread firmly together. Trim the threads around
5mm (¼in) from the knot and conceal the ends among the petals.

5 Cut out a 4cm (1½in) diameter circle of felt and spread textile
adhesive round the outside, as shown. Stick the flower on top.

6 Choose a button to cover the gap in the flower centre. Attach the
button with a few stitches, starting and finishing on the back of the
flower (see page 24).

Tip
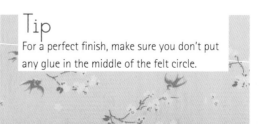
For a perfect finish, make sure you don't put
any glue in the middle of the felt circle.

Flower 2

This is a more complicated version of flower 1 with the top petals assembled in a spiral, but it is still easy to make.

Materials: 24 circles of fabric 5cm (2in) in diameter, for example 12 burgundy, 6 dark red and 6 fuchsia, one felt circle 5–6cm (2–2¼in) in diameter and one button at least 2–2.5cm (¾–1in) in diameter

Size of finished flower: about 8cm (3¼in) in diameter

1 Fold each circle of fabric in half. Use your nail to press the fold. If the fabric has a right and wrong side, make sure you fold it wrong sides together.

2 Thread a needle with around 50cm (20in) of doubled thread. Tie a knot in the end. Starting 5mm (¼in) from the edge, bring the needle up through the first base petal (burgundy), leaving around 5cm (2in) of the knotted end sticking out. Sew running stitches spaced around 2mm (⅛in) apart all round the curved edge. Finish with the needle and thread underneath.

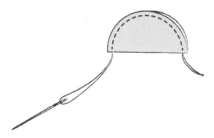

3 Using the same thread, continue in the same way along the curved edge of each of the other eleven remaining base petals (burgundy), always starting and finishing underneath the petal. Pull the thread to gather the petals.

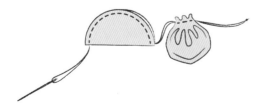

4 Knot the two ends of thread firmly together to hold the bases of the twelve burgundy petals in place. Trim the thread around 5mm (¼in) from the knot. Distribute the gathers evenly. Cut out a circle of felt around 5–6cm (2–2¼in) in diameter. Spread textile adhesive round the outside of the circle and stick the base of the flower on top.

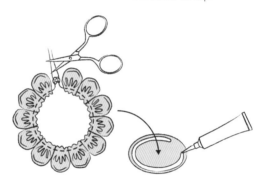

5 Using a new piece of thread, thread on the petals for the next (red) row and then the top (pink) row, forming the gathers as you go. Secure the thread firmly on the last one with a few stitches. Arrange into a spiral. Stitch through the first red petal then knot the two ends together. Stick the petals in place on the base.

6 Choose a button to cover the gap in the flower centre. Attach the button with a few stitches, starting and finishing on the back of the flower (see page 24).

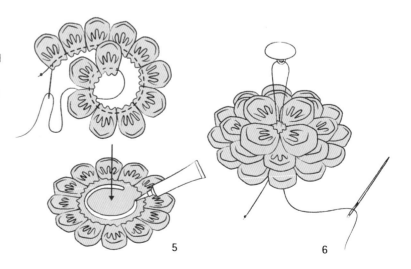

5

6

Flower 3

This flower's pointed petals rise in a delicate curve.

Materials: five circles of fabric 9cm (3¹/₂in) in diameter, one felt circle 3cm (1¹/₄in) in diameter and one button about 2.5cm (1in) in diameter

Size of finished flower: about 9cm (3¹/₂in) in diameter

1 Fold each circle of fabric in half. Use your nail to press the fold. If the fabric has a right and wrong side, make sure you fold it wrong sides together. Fold in half again, as shown, then arrange with the curved edge at the bottom.

2 Thread a needle with around 50cm (20in) of doubled thread. Tie a knot in the end. Starting 5mm (¹/₄in) from the edge, bring the needle up through the first petal, leaving around 5cm (2in) of the knotted end sticking out. Sew running stitches spaced about 2mm (¹/₈in) apart all round the curved edge. Finish with the needle and thread underneath.

3 Using the same thread, continue in the same way along the curved edge of each of the four remaining petals in the same direction, always starting and finishing underneath the petal. Pull the thread to gather the petals.

4 Knot the two ends of thread firmly together. Trim the threads around 5mm (¹/₄in) from the knot and conceal the ends among the petals.

5 Cut out a circle of felt around 3cm (1¹/₄in) in diameter. Spread textile adhesive round the outside of the circle and stick the flower on top.

6 Choose a button to cover the gap in the flower centre. Attach the button with a few stitches, starting and finishing on the back of the flower (see page 24).

Flower 4

This flower is made in the same way as flower 3, its double petals created by placing a small petal on top of each larger one.

Flower 5

This pretty star-shaped flower is made from circles of fabric folded three times.

Materials: five circles of fabric 7.5cm (3in) in diameter (yellow) and five circles of fabric 10.5cm (4¼in) in diameter (orange), one felt circle 5cm (2in) in diameter and one button about 5cm (2in) in diameter

Size of finished flower: about 13.5cm (5¼in) in diameter

1 Fold each circle of fabric in half, then in half again, as shown.

2 Centre the small petals over the large ones, making sure the folds go in the same direction. Thread a needle with around 50cm (20in) of doubled thread. Tie a knot in the end. Starting 5mm (¼in) from the edge, bring the needle up through the first petal, leaving around 5cm (2in) of the knotted end sticking out. Sew running stitches spaced around 2mm (⅛in) apart all round the curved edge, making sure the stitches go through all the layers. Finish with the needle and thread underneath.

3 Using the same thread, continue in the same way along the curved edge of each of the four remaining double petals, making sure they are pointing the same way and always starting and finishing underneath the petal.

4 Finish as for flower 3, using a piece of felt around 5cm (2in) in diameter.

Materials: six circles of fabric 9cm (3½in) in diameter, one felt circle 4cm (1½in) in diameter and one button about 3.5cm (1½in) in diameter

Size of finished flower: about 10.5cm (4¼in) in diameter

1 Fold each circle of fabric in half. Use your nail to press the fold. If the fabric has a right and wrong side, make sure you fold it wrong sides together. Fold in half again, then in half once more.

2 Assemble the petals and finish as for flower 3, using a piece of felt around 4cm (1½in) in diameter.

Tip

Make sure the folds on the petals are always pointing in the same direction during assembly.

Flower 6

This simple, open flower, with its rounded petals, evokes the freshness of spring.

Materials: five 8cm (3¼in) squares of fabric, one felt circle 4cm (1½in) in diameter and one button about 3.5cm (1½in) in diameter

Size of finished flower: about 8.5cm (3¼in) in diameter

1 Fold each square of fabric in half diagonally to make a triangle. Use your nail to press the fold. If the fabric has a right and wrong side, make sure you fold it wrong sides together.

2 Thread a needle with around 50cm (20in) of doubled thread. Tie a knot in the end. Starting 5mm (¼in) from the edge, bring the needle up through the first petal, leaving around 5cm (2in) of the knotted end sticking out. Sew running stitches spaced around 2mm (⅛in) apart along the two shorter sides, as shown. Finish with the needle underneath.

3 With the same thread, continue in the same way along the two shorter sides of each of the four remaining petals, always starting and finishing underneath the petal.

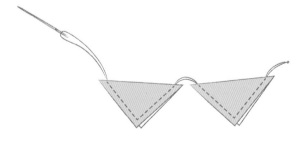

4 Pull the thread to gather the petals. Distribute the gathers evenly. Knot the two ends of thread firmly together. Trim the threads around 5mm (¼in) from the knot and conceal the ends among the petals.

5 Cut out a circle of felt around 4cm (1½in) in diameter. Spread textile adhesive round the outside of the circle and stick the flower on top.

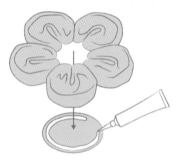

6 Choose a button to cover the gap in the flower centre. Attach the button with a few stitches, starting and finishing on the back of the flower (see page 24).

Flower 7

The prettily rimmed petals of this model meet in the centre, so a small pearl button or bead can be used for the flower's heart.

Materials: Seven 8cm (3¼in) squares of fabric, one felt circle 5cm (2in) and one button at least 5mm (¼in) in diameter

Size of finished flower: about 8cm (3¼in) in diameter

1 Fold each square of fabric in half diagonally to make a triangle. Use your nail to press the fold. If the fabric has a right and wrong side, make sure you fold it wrong sides together.

2 Fold the right and left hand points down to the bottom corner, as shown, creating a small square on its point.

3 Flip the whole thing over and fold the right and left corners in to meet at the centre, as shown.

4 Now fold the right side on to the left side. Cut off the bottom point at a right angle, as shown, then pin to hold the layers in place. Make six more petals in the same way.

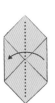 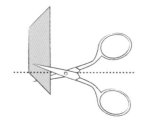 

5 Thread a needle with around 50cm (20in) of doubled thread. Tie a knot in the end. From right to left, push the needle through the pleat of the first petal, as shown, close to the bottom edge. Leave around 5cm (2in) of the knotted end sticking out.

6 Thread on the other petals in the same way. Pull on the thread to form a circle with the petals. Knot the two ends of thread firmly together. Trim the threads around 5mm (¼in) from the knot and conceal the ends among the petals.

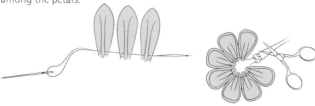

7 Cut out a circle of felt around 5cm (2in) in diameter. Spread textile adhesive round the outside of the circle, as shown, and stick the flower on top.

8 Choose a button or bead to cover the gap in the flower centre. Attach the button with a few stitches, starting and finishing on the back of the flower (see page 24).

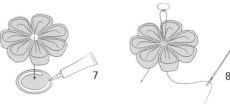

Flower 8

This variation of flower 7 has double petals, making for a stiffer flower and allowing for some subtle colour combinations.

Materials: seven 8cm (3¼in) squares of fabric (mauve) plus seven 7cm (2¾in) squares of fabric (pink), one felt circle 5cm (2in) in diameter and one button about 5mm (¼in) in diameter

Size of finished flower: about 8cm (3¼in) in diameter

For each petal, fold a square of each fabric in half diagonally to make a triangle. Place the smaller triangle on top of the larger one, centring it carefully, as shown. Then continue as for flower 7.

Flower 9

Bias binding elegantly highlights each
petal, like a delicate shadow added by a painter.

Materials: five 8cm (3¼in) squares of fabric and five pieces of bias
binding, each 11.5cm (4½in) long (total length: 57.5cm/22½in), one felt
circle 4cm (1½in) in diameter and one button at least 3cm (1¼in)
in diameter

Size of finished flower: about 8cm (3¼in) in diameter

1 Fold each square of fabric in half diagonally to make a triangle. Use
your nail to press the fold. If the fabric has a right and wrong side, make
sure you fold it wrong sides together.

2 Place a piece of folded bias binding along the long side of the triangle,
as shown. Fold the triangle in half and hold all the layers together at the
corner with a pin, as shown. Repeat with the remaining four squares.

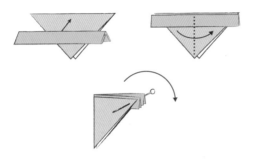

3 Thread a needle with around 50cm (20in) of doubled thread. Tie a knot
in the end. Starting 5mm (¼in) from the edge of the first triangle, push
the needle through where the pin is, leaving around 5cm (2in) of the
knotted end sticking out. Sew running stitches spaced around 2mm (⅛in)
apart along the long edge of the triangle, finishing with the needle and
thread underneath.

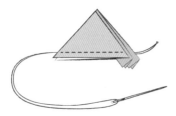

4 Using the same thread, continue in the same way along the base of
each of the four remaining petals, always starting and finishing
underneath the petal.

5 Pull the thread to gather the petals. Knot the two ends of thread firml
together. Trim the threads around 5mm (¼in) from the knot and conceal
the ends among the petals.

6 Cut out a circle of felt around 4cm (1½in) in diameter. Spread textile
adhesive round the outside of the circle and stick the flower on top,
as shown.

7 Choose a button to cover the gap in the flower centre. Attach the
button with a few stitches, starting and finishing on the back of the
flower (see page 24).

Flower 10

Reminiscent of a star anise, this two-colour flower can be made with a varying number of petals. The clever way in which it is constructed means that the contrast colour is on one side of each petal only, like a shadow.

Materials: ten 7.5cm (3in) squares of fabric in two different colours (orangey yellow and scarlet), one felt circle 4cm (1½in) and one button at least 2cm (¾in) in diameter
Size of finished flower: about 11cm (4¼in) in diameter

1 Fold a square of the main fabric in half diagonally to make a triangle. Use your nail to press the fold. If the fabric has a right and wrong side, make sure you fold it wrong sides together. Fold a square of the second fabric in the same way and then fold again.

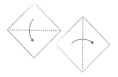

2 Place the second triangle, with the fold to the top, on the right side of the first triangle, as shown. Fold the first triangle over the second. Fold the bottom corner up to the top. Hold the petal in place by oversewing with a single piece of thread. Make all the petals in the same way.

3 Cut each petal in half.

4 Cut out a circle of felt around 4cm (1½in) in diameter. Dab adhesive on the points of the petals and place them on the felt to form your flower.

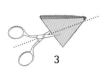 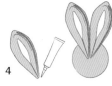

5 Choose a button to cover the gap in the flower centre. Attach the button with a few stitches, starting and finishing on the back of the flower (see page 24).

Flower 11

This variation of flower 10 is folded so that the contrast colour appears all round each petal.

Materials: nine 7.5cm (3in) squares of fabric in two different colours (orange and dark red), one felt circle 4cm (1½in) in diameter and one button at least 2cm (¾in) in diameter
Size of finished flower: about 11cm (4¼in) in diameter

1 Fold a square of each colour in half diagonally to make a triangle. Use your nail to press the fold. If the fabric has a right and wrong side, make sure you fold it wrong sides together. Fold each triangle in half again, placing the folds of the triangles in the outside fabric (dark red) to the left and the folds in the inside fabric (orange) to the right. Put an orange triangle on top of each dark red one.

  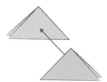

2 Fold again. Hold the petal in place by oversewing with a single piece of thread, as shown. Make all the petals in the same way. Finish as for flower 10.

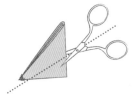

Tip
If the felt circle between the petals shows through, try clipping it into a star shape.

Clover® kanzashi flower makers are readily available onilne and can help you create a number of pretty flowers with ease. There are five shapes, each of which comes in three sizes. Choose the extra small size for flowers 3.5cm (1½in) in diameter, small for flowers of 5cm (2in) or large for 7.5cm (3in) flowers.

Flower 14
This is made with the gathered petal maker.

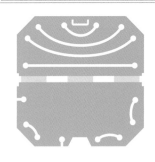 

Flower 12
This is made with the round petal maker.

Flower 15
This is made with the daisy petal maker.

Flower 13
This is made with the orchid petal maker.

Flower 16
This is made with the pointed petal maker.

Using a flower maker

The flower makers are all used in the same, whichever model you are making. They all have a central hinge and notches that act as guides for sewing the gathered petals.

1 Fold your fabric in half and close the flower maker over it, so that the fold of the fabric lies along the hinge.

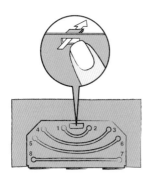

2 Cut the fabric around the template.

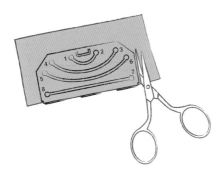

3 Thread a needle and stitch in the order marked on the template. Once you have completed all the stitches, remove the fabric and pull on the thread to gather the petal.

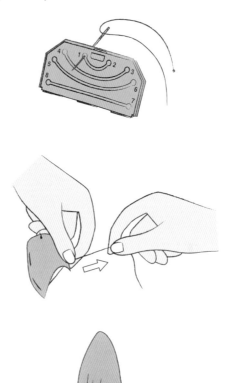

4 Without cutting the thread, make the other petals in the same way. To finish, gather the petals into a flower and make several small stitches on the back to secure them.

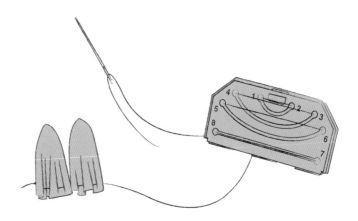

Tip

Make a test flower first using scrap fabric of a similar weight to the fabric you want to use for your flower.

Yo-yo

1 Cut out a cardboard template of double the diameter of the finished yo-yo (Suffolk puff), and use it to cut out a circle of fabric. Turn under the edge of your fabric circle by 5mm (¼in) all the way round.

2 Thread a needle with around 50cm (20in) of doubled thread. Tie a knot in the end. Bring the needle through the hem 2mm (⅛in) from the edge, leaving around 5cm (2in) of the knotted end sticking out. Sew small running stitches spaced about 2mm (⅛in) apart around the whole circle. Bring the thread out next to the first stitch.

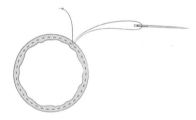

3 Pull the thread to form the gathers in the yo-yo. Knot the two ends of thread firmly together and trim the ends off short.

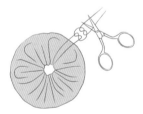

Yo-yo makers

These consist of two round parts that fit inside each other, trapping the fabric between them. You then simply cut out the fabric, leaving a margin, and sew round the margin following the marks. Yo-yos are finished in the same way as the other flowers. Yo-yo makers can also be used to make pumpkins.

Pumpkin

1 Using a cardboard template about twice the size of the finished pumpkin, cut out a circle of fabric. Thread a needle with around 50cm (20in) of doubled thread. Tie a knot in the end. Bring the needle through 2mm (⅛in) from the edge of the circle, leaving around 5cm (2in) of the knotted end sticking out. Sew small running stitches spaced about 2mm (⅛in) apart around the whole circle.

2 Bring the thread out next to the first stitch. Pull the thread to gather partially. Stuff and gather fully, ensuring the fabric is carefully packed to obtain a compact ball. Knot the two ends of thread firmly together and trim the ends off short.

3 Thread a needle with 50cm (20in) of doubled embroidery thread in a contrasting colour. Tie a knot in the end. Push the needle right through the ball, passing through the middle of the gathers and coming out in the centre of the other side. Bring the thread down round the side, insert in the base and bring it up through the centre once again; pull. Bring the thread down round the opposite side and insert again. Continue in this way until you have created six to eight segments. Sew a bead or button on top, making sure the stitches pass right through the pumpkin.

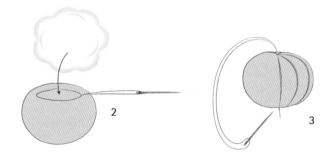

2

3

Pearl

Make a pearl following steps 1–2 for the pumpkin, using a fabric circle about twice as large as the desired pearl.

Rosette

1 You will need 20–30cm (8–12in) of satin ribbon, depending on how wide it is and how gathered you want it to be. Thread a needle with around 40cm (16in) of doubled thread. Tie a knot in the end. Sew along one long side, taking 2mm (⅛in) running stitches and leaving around 5cm (2in) of the knotted end hanging out. Start and finish on the back, 5mm (¼in) from the ends.

2 Pull the thread to gather the rosette. Knot the two ends of the thread together firmly and trim the ends close to the knot. Place the two ends of the ribbon together with right sides facing, and sew them in place with another thread. Finish by oversewing on the last stitch.

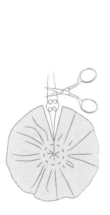

Finishing techniques

Pearl beads, buttons, lace flowers, jewellery findings and elements recycled from costume jewellery will give your kanzashi flowers added style and individuality. Here are some ideas to get you started.

Buttons

Buttons with shanks are easy to attach. Thread a needle and knot the end. Bring the needle up through the felt in the centre of the flower and pass it through the button shank. Pass it back through the felt, then through the shank again. Repeat until the button is secure. To finish, bring the needle out underneath the flower and make a knot by pushing the needle through the threads under the button and then pulling it through the resulting loop of thread. Trim off the thread end.

Buttons with holes are a good choice, but this time you need to think about thread colour. Either match it to the button or choose a pretty contrast. Thread a needle and knot the end. Position the button in the centre of the flower. Bring the needle up from underneath and through one of the holes in the button, pull the thread through and then push the needle down through the second hole in the button so it comes out underneath the flower. Repeat until the button is secure and then knot off as explained above. If the button has four holes you can sew in a cross, which works well for a flower centre, or in two parallel stitches.

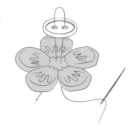

Self-cover buttons enable you to match a fabric. Simply follow the manufacturer's instructions to cover them. You can also use reclaimed buttons with shanks. In this case, cut out a circle of fabric, with a diameter about 1cm (³⁄₈in) bigger than the button to be covered. Thread a needle with doubled thread and tie a knot in the end. Sew 2mm (¹⁄₈in) running stitches around the circumference of the fabric circle, 3mm (about ¹⁄₈in) from the edge, and leaving 3cm (1¹⁄₄in) of the knotted end hanging out. Position the button face down in the middle of the fabric. Pull on the thread to gather the fabric around the button and then knot the two ends of the thread together.

Other decorations

Small plastic flowers, lace flowers or even crocheted flowers all work well at the centre of your kanzashi flowers. Depending on their shape and what they are made of, most decorations can be sewn on like a button or using a few discreet stitches. If they only have one hole, like the plastic flowers shown opposite, bring the thread up from the bottom, thread on a bead and then go back through the hole in the flower. The bead stops the thread from slipping back through the hole.

Stacked kanzashi flowers

A small kanzashi flower can be placed on top of a larger one to create a flower with more petals. The bottom flower is stuck to a felt base and the second flower glued on to the first. You can create many-layered flowers in this way. The buttons or other decorations are sewn on by stitching through all the layers.

Jewellery-making techniques

Jump rings make it possible to attach different items together. To hang a flower from a chain or cord, sew a jump ring (or two opposite each other) on to the back of the flower, passing the thread through the edge of the felt base.

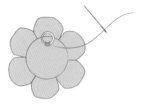

Use jewellery pliers to open and close jump rings, if necessary.

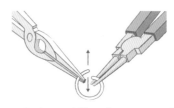

Head pins can also be used. Thread one or several beads on to a head pin to make a bead stop, or on to an eye pin to make a bead connector. Using wire cutters, snip off the pin about 8mm (scant ³⁄₈in) above the last bead and form a ring using round-nose jewellery pliers, as shown.

Assorted buttons, beads, jewellery findings and costume
jewellery elements to add to your kanzashi flowers

Projects

By simply experimenting with fabrics, adjusting sizes, stacking them and trying various combinations, you can create some beautiful kanzashi flowers to use in a host of ways, from decorations on bags or tiebacks to brooches and earrings.

Perfect as table decorations or sewn on to curtain tiebac
these beautiful water lilies are created using one flower
different sizes, and stacked to create a multi-petal flowe

Materials

* Silk fabric in the colours listed for each flower:

Pink-and-gold water lily: 15 × 80cm (6 × 31½in) of dark pink, 15 × 80cm
(6 × 31½in) of light pink, 10 × 70cm (4 × 27½in) of yellow ochre and
8 × 30cm (3¼ × 12in) of white

Small water lily on a leaf: 15 × 80cm (6 × 31½in) of dark pink, 10 × 70cm
(4 × 27½in) of light pink, 8 × 30cm (3¼ × 12in) of white and 15 × 30cm
(6 × 12in) of green

Large water lily on a leaf: 10 × 70cm (4 × 27½in) of white, 25 × 80cm
(10 × 31½in) of light pink, 8 × 30cm (3¼ × 12in) of dark pink and
18 × 34cm (7 × 13½in) of green

* 4 craft stamens, depending on the model: two-colour red and white
or plain white
* Matching felt to cover the back
* Textile adhesive

Pink-and-gold water lily

Following the instructions on page 14 for flower 3, but using the
dimensions in the cutting guide below, make the four layers of petals.
You can vary the way the petals sit in each layer, as shown in the
photograph. To close the yellow corolla, position the petals so that they
overlap and pull the gathers very tight.

Stick the biggest flower on to the felt base then stick the others on top in
size order, ending with the smallest flower.

CUTTING GUIDE

* Bottom layer, flower 3: 6 dark pink petals each made from a 10.5cm
(4¼in) diameter circle of fabric
* Middle layer, flower 3: 6 light pink petals each made from a 10.5cm
(4¼in) diameter circle
* Top layer, flower 3: 6 yellow-ochre petals each made from an 8.5cm
(3¼in) diameter circle
* Centre, flower 3: 5 white petals each made from a 5cm (2in)
diameter circle
* Felt base: 6cm (2¼in) diameter circle

Tip

To make a quick curtain tieback, sew or stick
your water lily to a broad ribbon.

Small water lily on a leaf

Flower Following the instructions on page 14 for flower 3 but using the dimensions in the cutting guide below, make the three layers of petals. You can vary the way the petals sit in each layer, as shown in the photograph. Stick the flowers on top of each other in size order with a bit of textile adhesive. Slide the stems of the stamens into the central hole. Bend the stems and sew them into place with a few stitches. Stick the felt circle to the back of the flower to neaten the back.

Leaf Fold the rectangle of green silk in half with right sides facing and pin to hold. Cut the leaf pattern through both layers, using the pattern on page 78. Keep the two layers pinned together and sew all round, about 5mm (^{1}/$_4$in) from the edge, going around the slit and leaving an opening in one side for turning out. Cut along the slit. Turn the leaf right side out. Sew up the opening using small stitches. Stick the flower on to the leaf.

CUTTING GUIDE

- Bottom layer, flower 3: 6 dark pink petals each made from a 10.5cm (4^1/$_4$in) diameter circle of fabric
- Middle layer, flower 3: 6 light pink petals each made from a 7.5cm (3in) diameter circle
- Top layer, flower 3: 5 white petals each made from a 5cm (2in) diameter circle
- Felt base: 5cm (2in) diameter circle

Large water lily on a leaf

Make this in the same way as the small water lily on a leaf but for the bottom layer, which has a two-colour flower, follow the instructions for flower 4 on page 15.

CUTTING GUIDE

- Bottom layer, flower 4: 6 white petals each made from a 12cm (4^3/$_4$in) diameter circle of fabric and 6 pink petals, each made from a 10.5cm (4^1/$_4$in) diameter circle
- Middle layer, flower 3: 6 pink petals each made from a 7.5cm (3in) diameter circle
- Top layer, flower 3: 5 dark pink petals each made from a 5cm (2in) diameter circle
- Felt base: 5cm (2in) diameter circle

Cherry Blossom

In Japanese culture, the cherry blossom is a symbol of the beauty and fragility of life. But for you, the beauty can last forever with these gorgeous fabric versions.

Materials

FOR THE BROOCH

• Fabrics: 8 × 40cm (3¹/₄ × 16in) of white silk and 8 × 30cm (3¹/₄ × 12in) of green silk
• Jewellery-making filigree wire, around 1.5cm (¹/₂in) in diameter
• 1.5cm (¹/₂in) bead or button
• Brooch mount, around 3cm (1¹/₄in) long
• Pink felt for the base
• Textile adhesive

FOR THE NECKLACE

• Fabric: 10 × 40cm (4 × 16in) of pink poplin, 8 × 30cm (3¹/₄ × 12in) of dark green taffeta, 8 × 30cm (3¹/₄ × 12in) of yellow cotton with white spots, 10 × 15cm (4 × 6in) of Japanese-style cotton fabric (use more if needed to centre the patterns)
• Eight 3mm (¹/₄in) pearly beads
• 1m rouleau cord (39in) made from Liberty cotton (or you could use a length of jewellery cord)
• Stuffing for the pumpkins
• Pink felt for the bases
• Textile adhesive

White brooch

Flower Using the measurements in the cutting guide below, and following the instructions for flower 7, steps 1–4 on page 17, prepare 5 white petals. Follow the instructions on page 19 for flower 11 to prepare 5 green petals for the leaves, but only use one layer of fabric. Complete the first white petal then thread on a leaf. Continue threading on the petals and leaves alternately. Finish off as for flower 7. Thread a needle and bring it up from the back of the flower through the flower centre, through the filigree and then the bead, then back through the filigree and flower; repeat to secure the centre. Knot the thread and trim the ends.

Finishing Sew the brooch mount on to the back of the flower, positioning it slightly above the central point. Pinch the end of each petal with your fingers to make the tip fold inwards, as shown below.

CUTTING GUIDE

• Petals, flower 7: 5 white petals each made from a 6cm (2¹/₄in) square of fabric
• Leaves, flower 11 (single layer): 5 green petals each made from a 5cm (2in) square of fabric
• Felt base: 3cm (1¹/₄in) diameter circle

Shaping the petals

Shape your petals by pinching them as shown below. This is all you need to do with crisp fabrics such as silk or firm poplin. If your fabric is softer, apply a small amount of adhesive with a pin into each pinched fold.

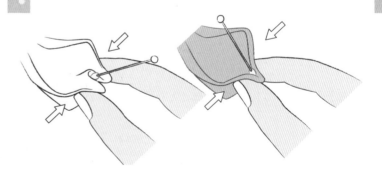

Flower necklace

Central flower Using the measurements in the cutting guide below, and following the instructions for flower 7, steps 1–4 on page 17, prepare 5 pink petals. Follow the instructions on page 19 for flower 11 to prepare 5 green petals for the leaves but only use one layer of fabric. Complete the first pink petal then thread on a leaf. Continue threading on the petals and leaves alternately. To make the flower centre, make a yellow flower following the instructions for flower 13 (see page 20). Stick the large flower on to the felt base, only applying adhesive round the edge of the felt, then stick the small yellow flower on top. Sew a bead into the centre, like a button, then sew another five around it.

CUTTING GUIDE FOR THE CENTRAL FLOWER
• Petals, flower 7: 5 pink petals each made from a 7.5cm (3in) square of fabric
• Leaves, flower 11 (single layer): 5 green leaves each made from a 6cm (2¹/₄in) square of fabric
• Heart, flower 13: 5 yellow petals made using the very-small size orchid petal maker
• Felt base: 5cm (2in) diameter circle

Pumpkins Follow the instructions on page 22 using two circles of fabric, 6cm (2¹/₄in) in diameter, ensuring that any pattern is centred. Sew a pearl bead in the centre of each.

Assembly Centre the flower on the rouleau cord with one point facing up and two petals on the cord. Attach the flower to the cord by stitching through the felt base and then add a few stitches at the end of the two petals. Sew a pumpkin on to each side. This necklace simply knots round your neck. You can also wear it in your hair.

Ring

Make the flower following the instructions for the brooch on page 32 but using the dimensions in the cutting guide below. Stick the crocheted flower in the centre, then stick the flower on to the ring mount using strong multi-purpose glue.

CUTTING GUIDE

• Petals, flower 7: 5 patterned petals each made from a 5cm (2in) square of fabric (cut carefully from patterned fabric to create the look shown)
• Leaves, flower 11 (single layer): 5 yellow petals each made from a 4cm (1½in) square
• Felt base: 3cm (1¼in) diameter circle

Cloche

Find a suitable branch. Make the number of flowers desired, following the instructions for flower 1 on page 12: each flower should have four white or pink petals each made from a 3cm (1¼in) diameter fabric circle. A felt base isn't needed because these flowers are so small. Sew a pearl bead into the centre of each flower. Arrange the flowers attractively on the branch and glue into place. Wedge the end of the branch into the groove in the base before putting the glass cloche in place. If necessary, trim the end of the branch slightly.

Materials

FOR THE RING

• 8 × 30cm (3¼ × 12in) of pink-and-white cotton fabric, ideally with a Japanese-style pattern and 6 × 30cm (2¼ × 12in) of yellow poplin
• Small crocheted flower or button, 1.5–2cm (½–¾in) in diameter
• Flat-topped ring blank
• Pink felt
• Strong multi-purpose glue

FOR THE CLOCHE

• Glass cloche
• Small, suitably shaped branch that will fit inside the cloche
• 6 × 6cm (2¼ × 2¼in) of pink or white silk for each flower
• 3mm (¼in) pearly bead for each flower
• Multi-purpose glue

Funky Flowers

These cheerful 1970s-inspired designs are lots of fun, with bold contrasting colours and simple shapes. Stitch the large flower to the smart clutch bag or attach it to brooch back and make the matching earrings to comple the look.

Materials

FOR THE FLOWER

- Fabrics: 12 × 70cm (4³/₄ × 27¹/₂in) of dark orange cotton, 10 × 60cm (4 × 23³/₄in) of light orange cotton sateen, 12 × 35cm (4³/₄ × 13³/₄in) of blue silk and 12 × 30cm (4³/₄ × 12in) of purple taffeta
- 3.5cm (1¹/₂in) self-cover button covered with a coordinating fabric (see page 24)
- Orange felt
- Textile adhesive

FOR THE CLUTCH BAG

- 28 × 42cm (11 × 16¹/₂in) of purple cotton sateen, 28 × 42cm (11 × 16¹/₂in) of light orange cotton sateen and 28 × 42cm (11 × 16¹/₂in) of cotton wadding
- 60cm (23¹/₂in) of old-gold chain around 5mm (¹/₄in) wide
- 1m (1yd) of turquoise satin ribbon around 3mm (¹/₄in) wide

Clutch bag

Flower Make each leaf individually following the instructions for flower 11 on page 19 but using the measurements in the cutting guide below. Arrange them in a plume and hold them in place with a few stitches or a bit of adhesive. Assemble the petals following the instructions for flower 8 on page 17. Slide the leaves between two of the petals. Stick the whole thing on to the felt base. Sew the covered button into the middle.

CUTTING GUIDE FOR THE FLOWER

- Leaves, flower 11: three turquoise petals each made from a 10.5cm (4¹/₄in) square of fabric plus three purple petals each made from a 9.5cm (3³/₄in) square
- Petals, flower 8: six dark orange petals each made from a 10.5cm (4¹/₄in) square of fabric plus six light orange petals each made from an 8cm (3¹/₄in) square
- Felt base: 5cm (2in) diameter circle

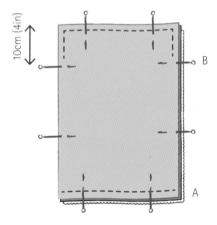

Making the clutch bag

1 Lay the purple outer fabric right side up on top of the wadding, then place the orange lining right side down on top. Sew along one of the shorter edges (A), taking a 1cm (³/₈in) seam allowance. Sew the flap, as shown in the diagram, starting and finishing 10cm (4in) from the short edge (B), again with a 1cm (³/₈in) seam allowance.

Tip

If you want the flower to be detachable, sew a 5cm (2in) brooch mount on to the back, positioning it slightly above the centre.

2 Separate and fold the layers of fabric carefully, bringing stitching line A up to the bottom of the flap stitching (B) as shown. Sew round the outside, leaving a 5mm (¹⁄₄in) opening 5mm (¹⁄₄in) from the flap stitching on both sides where the chain will be inserted. Sew round the lining, leaving an opening 8cm (3¹⁄₄in) from the fold on one side. Turn the clutch bag right sides out through this opening and then sew up the gap using small stitches.

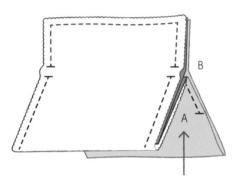

3 Thread the ribbon through the links of the chain. Insert the ends of the chain into the small side openings on the bag and sew securely in place. Sew the flower on to the flap, making sure the needle passes through both the bag and the felt base.

****

Materials

FOR THE EARRINGS

• 10 × 20cm (4 × 8in) of orange cotton sateen
• Two 6mm (¼in) metallic buttons or beads
• Two bronze earring mounts
• Two 8mm (³⁄₈in) jump rings
• Jewellery pliers
• Orange felt
• Textile adhesive

****

Funky earrings

Make two flowers, following the instructions on page 12 for flower 1
with five petals each made from a 3cm (1¼in) fabric circle. Stick them on
to a felt base around 2cm (¾in) in diameter. Sew a button to the centre
of each flower. Stitch a jump ring on the back, on the edge of the felt.
Using jewellery pliers, fix the earring mount on to the jump ring.

The combination of dark satin, cotton and metallic fabric give a wonderfully old-fashioned look to these charming flowers. Carefully chosen metal or plastic jewellery findings complete this elegant style.

Materials

FOR THE COLLAR

- Fabrics: 30 × 30cm (12 × 12in) of mustard yellow cotton with white spots for the collar and 45 × 30cm (18 × 12in) of purple cotton sateen for the collar and flower
- 7cm (2³/₄in) of gold bias binding for the flower
- Hook-and-eye fasteners
- 1cm (³/₈in) blue flower bead
- Black or purple felt for the flower base
- Textile adhesive

Peter Pan collar

Flower Following the instructions on page 14 for flower 3 and using the dimensions given in the cutting guide below, make the ring of purple sepals and stick it to the felt base. Following the instructions on page 23, make a gold rosette from the gold bias binding, leaving the binding folded. Add a dab of adhesive to the sepals and stick the rosette on top. Finally, stitch the blue flower bead on top.

CUTTING GUIDE FOR THE FLOWER

- Sepals, flower 3: 7 purple petals each made from a 5.5cm (2¹/₄in) diameter circle of fabric
- Petals, rosette: 7cm (2³/₄in) of gold bias binding
- Felt base: 2cm (³/₄in) diameter circle

Making the collar

1 Fold the yellow fabric rectangle in half, right sides together. Trace the pattern on page 79 and place your new pattern on the fabric, along the fold as indicated. Cut out the shape through both layers then unfold the complete collar top. Repeat with the purple fabric to cut the under-collar. Pin the two collar pieces right sides together and sew 5mm (¹/₄in) from edge, leaving an opening at the back between the two points marked on the pattern. Clip into the seam allowance on the curves. Turn right side out through the opening and close up with small stitches.

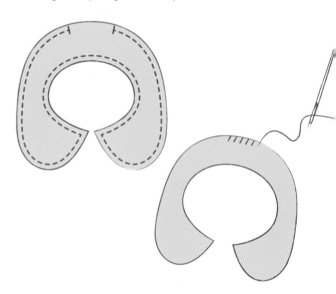

2 Sew on the hook-and-eye sections at the points marked, where the two sides of the collar overlap. Stitch the flower at one end of the collar, close to the edge so that when the collar is closed it is central. Make sure the needle passes through the felt base.

Materials

FOR THE BROOCH

- Fabrics: 9 × 60cm (3½in × 23½in) of purple taffeta and 8 × 30cm (3¼ × 12in) of striped taffeta
- 80cm (31½in) of gold bias binding
- 1cm (⅜in) blue flower bead
- Brooch mount, around 2.5cm (1in) long
- Black or purple felt for the base
- Textile adhesive

FOR THE BRACELET

- Fabrics: 9 × 20cm (3½ × 8in) of purple taffeta and 8 × 30cm (3¼ × 12in) of striped taffeta
- Bronze filigree flower, around 1.5cm (½in) in diameter
- 5mm (¼in) purple cabochon
- Leather or cord strap and clasp to fit the strap
- Textile and multi-purpose glue

FOR THE HEADBAND

- Fabrics: 10 × 50cm (4 × 20in) of striped taffeta, 15 × 30cm (6 × 12in) of purple taffeta and 7 × 20cm (2¾ × 8in) of brown taffeta
- Two 3cm (1¼in) bronze filigree flowers
- 8mm (scant ⅜in) purple cabochon
- 1cm (⅜in) purple flower bead
- Bronze-coloured headband
- Black or purple felt
- Textile and multi-purpose glue

Brooch

Following the instructions on page 18 and using the dimensions in the cutting guide below, make flower 9 from the purple fabric and gold binding. Make a striped flower following the instructions for flower 3 on page 14 but using the dimensions below. Glue the larger flower to the felt then glue the striped flower on top and sew the bead into the centre. Sew the brooch mount on to the back of the flower, positioning it slightly above the central point.

CUTTING GUIDE

- Sepals, flower 9: 7 purple petals each made from a 7.5cm (3in) purple square of fabric plus gold bias binding
- Petals, flower 3: 5 striped taffeta petals each made from a 5.5cm (2in) diameter circle of fabric
- Felt base: 4cm (1½in) diameter circle

Bracelet

Using the measurements in the cutting guide below, make the purple leaves following the instructions for flower 11 on page 19 but using only one layer of fabric. Make the ring of sepals following the instructions for flower 3 on page 14 but using the fabric dimensions below. Cut the leather strap to the size you want for your bracelet, taking into account the length of the clasp. Put adhesive on the two ends of the strap and insert them into each part of the clasp. Stick the sepals in place on the strap then add the petals. Stick the filigree flower and cabochon in the centre of the flower.

CUTTING GUIDE

- Leaves, flower 11: 2 purple petals (single layer) each made from a 7cm (2¾in) square of fabric
- Sepals, flower 3: 5 striped petals each made from a 5cm (2in) diameter circle of fabric

Headband

Using the measurements in the cutting guide below, make the flowers following the instructions for flower 3 on page 14. Refer to the photograph to arrange the colours. Stick the flowers on to the felt bases. Sew the filigree flowers into the centre. Sew the flower bead into the middle of the big flower and glue the cabochon into the centre of the small one. Sew or glue the flowers on to the headband.

CUTTING GUIDE FOR THE LARGE FLOWER

- Sepals, flower 3: 6 petals, each made from a 7.5cm (3in) diameter circle of fabric
- Petals, flower 3: 6 petals, each made from a 6cm (2¼in) diameter circle of fabric (3 brown and 3 purple)
- Felt base: 3cm (1¼in) diameter circle

CUTTING GUIDE FOR THE SMALL FLOWER

- Sepals, flower 3: 7 purple petals, each made from a 5cm (2in) diameter circle of fabric
- Felt base: 2cm (¾in) diameter circle

Spring Flowers

Fresh as a daisy, these simple flowers are quick to make and sure to impress. Pop them on a pouch, use one for a ring or bracelet, or even make a whole bunch for a decorative display.

****

Materials

FOR THE POUCH

• Fabric for the flowers: 8 × 40cm (3¼ × 16in) of coral pink cotton sateen, 8 × 30cm (3¼ × 12in) of coral pink cotton with white spots, 5 × 20cm (2 × 8in) of coral pink cotton with yellow spots and 5 × 5cm (2 × 2in) of yellow cotton with white spots (or the fabrics of your choice)

• Fabric for the bag: 22 × 16cm (8½ × 6¼in) of silver lame for the outside and 22 × 16cm (8½ × 6¼in) of cotton fabric for the lining in the colour of your choice

• Light grey felt to back the flowers

• 5mm (¼in) fluorescent bead for the smallest flower centre

• 1cm (½in) yellow flower bead for the middle-sized flower centre

• 20cm (8in) pink zip

• Mobile phone charm with a lobster clasp and three 5mm (¼in) fluorescent beads for the zip tag (optional)

****

Zip-up pouch

The flowers Make the flowers for the bag following the instructions for flower 1 on page 12 but using the dimensions listed in the cutting guide below. Make the large flower from pink cotton and stick it to the grey felt base. Make a fabric pearl from the yellow spotted fabric following the instructions on page 22 and using a circle of yellow spotted fabric 3cm (1¼in) in diameter. Make the medium and small flowers following the instructions for flower 1, again referring to the cutting guide below for sizing. Cut small circles of felt to neaten the back of the two smaller flowers. Sew the flower bead into the centre of the medium flower and the fluorescent bead into the centre of the small flower.

CUTTING GUIDE FOR THE FLOWERS

Large flower, flower 1: 5 petals, each made from a 6cm (2¼in) diameter circle of pink sateen

Pearl for the large flower made from a 3cm (1¼in) circle of yellow fabric

Large flower base: 2cm (¾in) diameter circle of grey felt

Medium flower, flower 1: 5 petals each made from a 5cm (2in) circle of pink fabric with white spots

Small flower, flower 1: 5 petals each made from a 3cm (1¼in) circle of pink fabric with yellow spots

Making the pouch

1 Place the zip right sides together with one silver fabric rectangle, aligning the edge with the long edge of fabric. Using a zip foot on your sewing machine, sew the zip in place, stopping 1cm (⅜in) from each end.

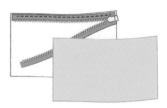

2 Pin a rectangle of lining material, right side down on top, so it is facing the wrong side of the zip and sew on as in step 1. Your fabric rectangles should be aligned.

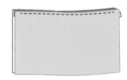

3 Repeat steps 1 and 2 on the other side of the zip with the two other fabric rectangles.

4 Open the zip halfway. Pin the two silver rectangles together, right sides facing. Sew up the three sides. Pin the two rectangles of the lining together, right sides together. Sew up the three sides, but leave a 10cm (4in) opening in the middle of the long edge. Turn the bag the out through the opening and sew up the gap with small stitches.

5 Sew the flowers on to one side of the bag. Thread three beads on to the mobile phone charm and knot to secure them. Clip the charm on to the zip pull.

Materials

FOR THE BRACELET

- 6 × 30cm (2¼ × 12in) of yellow cotton with white spots
- 1cm (⅜in) pink flower bead
- Four 5mm (¼in) fluorescent beads
- Silver findings: 4 jump rings, 4 eye pins, a lobster clasp and around 12cm (4¾in) of silver chain with medium-sized links
- Round-nose and flat-nose jewellery pliers
- Yellow felt
- Textile adhesive

FOR THE RING

- 6 × 30cm (2¼ × 12in) of hot orange cotton with yellow spots
- 1cm (⅜in) yellow flower bead
- Silver flat-top ring blank
- Yellow felt
- Textile and multi-purpose glue

FOR THE VASE DECORATION

- Fabrics: 20 × 40cm (8 ×16in) of yellow spotty cotton, 15 × 35cm (6 × 13¾in) of red cotton sateen and 10 × 10cm (4 × 4in) of pink satin or cotton sateen
- Fabric to go around the vase: 13cm (5in) × perimeter of the vase + 2cm (¾in)
- Yellow felt
- Textile adhesive

Bracelet

Flower Follow the instructions for flower 3 on page 14 to make the flower using 4cm (1½in) circles of fabric. Stick the petals to a felt base 2cm (¾in) in diameter. Sew the flower bead into the centre of the flower.

Assembly On the back of the flower, sew two jump rings on opposite sides of the felt circle, as shown. Mount the beads on eye pins to make bead connectors (see page 24). Cut the chain and join it to the bead connectors and the jump rings on the back of the flower as shown in the illustration. Adjust the length so it fits your wrist and fit the chain to the lobster clasp with a jump ring. The final jump ring can be added to the other end of the bracelet for the clasp to clip on to.

Ring

Make a flower as for the bracelet and stick it on to the ring mount.

Vase decoration

Flower Make all the parts of the flower using the dimensions in the cutting guide below. Make the yellow petals, following the instructions for flower 7 on page 17 and for the red petals see page 21. Make a pink yo-yo for the flower centre as explained on page 22. Dab glue round the outside of the felt base, stick on the first layer, then the second. Sew the centre in place, making sure the stitches go through the petals of the middle layer.

Fabric band Fold the strip of fabric lengthways, right sides together, pin and then sew along the long side. Turn right sides out. Fold one of the ends in by 1cm (⅜in). Slip the other end into the folded end to form a ring. Adjust the size to fit round the vase. Sew up using tiny stitches. Sew the flower on to the fabric band – you can sew it over the join to conceal it.

CUTTING GUIDE FOR THE FLOWER

- Large petals, flower 7: 8 yellow petals, each made from an 8cm (3¼in) diameter circle of fabric
- Medium petals: 9 red petals made using the small-size daisy petal maker
- Flower centre: pink yo-yo made with a yo-yo maker (finished size 2cm/¾in) or from a 6cm (2¼in) circle of fabric
- Felt base: 6.5cm (2½in) diameter circle

For the flowers in the vase, make any of the flowers you like in this book and glue each one to the end of a thin stick. Your lovely bouquet will last all year. Natural sticks give a realistic curve, but you can also use kebab skewers or florist's wire for the flower stems.

Tip
Use double-sided adhesive tape to secure the fabric ring on the vase.

Retro fabrics are always fun to use. These have a flavou of the 1950s, in shades of terracotta and blue. Add som bronze-coloured findings to create feminine and romantic accessories.

Materials

FOR THE NECKLACE

• Fabrics: 6 × 40cm (2¹/₄ × 16in) of blue cotton sateen, 6 × 40cm (2¹/₄ × 16in) of red flowery cotton voile and a scrap of blue and cream cotton
• Two 1.5cm (¹/₂in) enamelled filigree findings (blue and red)
• Three 0.5cm (¹/₄in) khaki glass beads
• Bronze findings: 4cm (1¹/₂in) bird cage with removable base; 80cm (31¹/₂in) flat chain, 5mm (¹/₄in) wide; a headpin; an eye pin; seven 8mm (³/₈in) jump rings and a lobster clasp
• 2cm (³/₄in) blue plastic flower
• 6 red seed beads for the cage decoration
• Felt
• Jewellery pliers
• Textile adhesive

FOR THE BROOCH

• Fabrics: 20 × 30cm (8 × 12in) patterned blue cotton and a scrap of fabric with a face on it
• 2.5cm (1in) self-cover button
• Brooch mount, around 2.5cm (1in) long
• Felt to back the flowers
• Textile adhesive

Necklace

The flowers Following the instructions for flower 7 on page 17, make two flowers with seven petals from 4.5cm (1³/₄in) fabric squares. Stick them on to a felt base around 2.5cm (1in) in diameter. In the centre of each flower, sew a filigree finding and a glass bead. Sew two jump rings on to the back, one on each side of the felt base.

The cage Make a yo-yo using a circle of fabric around 3cm (1¹/₄in) in diameter (see page 22). Thread the yo-yo on to the headpin, followed by the plastic flower, a glass bead and three seed beads. Attach the whole thing to the eye pin. Thread three seed beads on to the eye pin. Put the end of the pin through the hole on top of the cage and bend into a loop. Close the cage.

Assembling the necklace

Attach the cage to the centre of the chain with a jump ring. Attach the clasp parts to each end of the chain using a jump ring. Open the jump rings on the backs of the flowers and close them over the chain links to attach the flowers: the first should be around 7cm (2³/₄in) from the cage, the second 12cm (4³/₄in).

Brooch

Following the instructions for flower 6 on page 16, make a flower using 8cm (3¹/₄in) fabric circles for the petals. Cover the button with the fabric with the face on it and sew it to the flower centre. Sew the brooch mount to the felt on the back of the flower, positioning it slightly above the central point.

Tip

Don't worry if you cannot find the same fabrics and findings as used for the flowers shown. Your own choices will make the flowers much more personal to you.

Materials

FOR THE LEAF BROOCH

Fabrics: 10 × 60cm (4 × 23^1/$_2$in) of blue flowery cotton, 6 × 30cm (2^1/$_4$ × 12in) of blue cotton sateen and 7 × 15cm (2^3/$_4$ × 6in) of red cotton

1cm (^{3}/$_8$in) red flower bead

Brooch mount, around 3.5cm (1.5in) long

Matching felt for backing

Textile adhesive

FOR THE HAIR SLIDES

Fabric for the flowery hair slide: 35 × 8cm (13^3/$_4$ × 3^1/$_4$in) of blue cotton sateen, 35 × 8cm (13^3/$_4$ × 3^1/$_4$in) of patterned blue cotton plus a scrap of flowery red cotton

Fabric for the pumpkin hair slides: scraps of blue cotton sateen and red flowery cotton

Three coordinating seed beads

Three hair slides

Stuffing for the pumpkins

Textile adhesive

Leaf brooch

Referring to the instructions for flower 6 on page 16 and flower 7 on page 17, make the two layers of the flower using the dimensions in the cutting guide below. Stick the larger flower on the felt base and the smaller flower on top. Thread a needle and pass it through the base so it comes out on the edge of the felt. Make the first leaf (see page 14), gather it and sew back down through the base to fix it in position. Make the second leaf and attach it in the same way. Sew the flower button into the middle of the flower. Sew the brooch mount on to the back of the flower, positioning it slightly above the central point.

CUTTING GUIDE

- Bottom layer, flower 6: 7 blue patterned petals each made from a 7cm (2^3/$_4$in) fabric square
- Top layer, flower 7: 7 plain blue petals, each made from a 4cm (1^1/$_2$in) fabric square
- Leaves, flower 3: 2 red petals, each made from a 5cm (2in) diameter circle
- Felt base: 5cm (2in) diameter circle

Flower hair slide

Referring to the instructions for flower 8 on page 17, make the flower using the dimensions in the cutting guide below. Stick it to the felt base. Make the pumpkin following the instructions on page 22. To attach it to the flower centre, bring the needle up from the base of the flower, through the pumpkin, through the bead then back down through the pumpkin and base again. Repeat several times. Sew the flower to a hair slide.

CUTTING GUIDE

- Petals, flower 8: 6 petals, each made from a 5cm (2in) blue fabric square and a 4cm (1^1/$_2$in) patterned square
- Flower centre: red pumpkin made from a 4cm (1^1/$_2$in) fabric circle
- Felt base: 2cm (^{3}/$_4$in) in diameter

Pumpkin hair slides

Make each pumpkin from a fabric circle, 3–4cm (1^1/$_2$in) in diameter following the instructions on page 22 and then stitch each one to a hair slide.

With their pointed petals and Japanese-style fabrics, these stars have an exotic flavour. They make excellent wall decorations or could even be hung from a Christmas tree. Larger ones can be made into attractive trays for serving rolls or sweets.

Materials

FOR THE HANGINGS

• Fabric for the red-and-white hanging: 9 × 45cm (3¹/₂ × 17³/₄in) of Japanese-style cotton in two designs plus a scrap of plain red cotton
• Fabric for the blue-and-red hanging: 12 × 55cm (4³/₄ × 21³/₄in) of Japanese-style blue patterned cotton, 9 × 60cm (3¹/₂ × 23¹/₂in) of blue cotton sateen and a scrap of red patterned fabric for the button centre
• Fabric for the double star hanging: 9 × 50cm (3¹/₂ × 20in) of blue cotton sateen, 7 × 40cm (2³/₄ × 16in) of Japanese-style creamy cotton, 7 × 50cm (2³/₄ × 20in) of red Japanese-style fabric and a scrap of plain red cotton
• 15–30cm (6–12in) of rouleau cord or cotton cord, the length depending on the model
• Accessories depending on the model: 5mm (¹/₄in) metal shank button; 2cm (³/₄in) or 2.5cm (1in) self-cover button; 4.5cm (2in) plastic flower with a hole in the middle; small flower with a stem; cat-motif bell or decorative bead
• Matching felt for backing
• Textile adhesive

FOR THE BASKET

• Fabrics: 40 × 60cm (21¹/₂ × 23¹/₂in) of Japanese-style cotton fabric and 12 × 12cm (4³/₄ × 4³/₄in) of red spotty cotton
• 50cm (20in) of cotton cord, ribbon or lace
• 5.5cm (2in) diameter circle of thin card
• Matching felt for backing
• Textile adhesive

Red-and-white hanging

Referring to the instructions for flower 5 on page 15, and using the dimensions in the cutting guide below, make two five-petal flowers. Make the pumpkin following the instructions on page 22 using a 6cm (2¹/₄in) circle. Stick the first flower to the felt then stick the other one on the top with the petals between those of the bottom layer. To attach the pumpkin to the flower centre, bring the needle up from the base of the flower, through the pumpkin, through the bead then back down through the pumpkin and base again. Repeat several times. Sew the star on to a length of cord, so the cord extends above and below. Fold the cord at the top to form a hanging loop and sew into place. Sew a decorative bell on to the other end.

CUTTING GUIDE

• Lower layer, flower 5: 5 red petals, each made from a 7.5cm (3in) diameter circle of fabric
• Middle layer, flower 5: 5 patterned petals, each made from a 7.5cm (3in) diameter circle
• Flower centre: red pumpkin from a 6cm (2¹/₄in) diameter circle of fabric
• Felt base: 3.5cm (1.5in) diameter circle

Tip

Change the fabric colours to match your beads and findings or to fit in with a special occasion.

Double star hanging

Following the instructions for flower 5 on page 15 and flower 15 on pag
20, and using the dimensions in the cutting guide below, make the layers
for the large star. Pass the stem of the small flower through the plastic
flower, then into the centre of the star. Bend the stem and sew it into
place with a few stitches. Stick the felt circle to the back of the star to
neaten it. Make the small star following the instructions for flower 5 on
page 15 and using 7.5cm (3in) fabric squares. Sew a 2cm (³/₄in) self-
covered button into the centre. Stitch the large star to one end of the
cord and the small one in the middle. Stitch the free end of the fabric
cord into a hanging loop.

LARGE STAR CUTTING GUIDE
• Bottom layer, flower 5: 6 blue petals, each made from a 7.5cm (3in)
fabric square
• Top layer, flower 15: 8 red petals made using the small daisy
petal maker
• Felt base: 3cm (1¹/₄in) diameter circle

SMALL STAR CUTTING GUIDE
• Star, flower 5: 6 petals, each made from a 5cm (2in) diameter
fabric circle
• Felt base: 2cm (³/₄in) diameter circle

Blue-and-red hanging

Following the instructions for flower 5 on page 15 and flower 3 on page
14, and using the dimensions in the cutting guide below, make the two
fabric flowers. Assemble in the same way as the red-and-white hanging
(see page 52), replacing the pumpkin with a 2.5cm (1in) self-covered
button, and using a bead on the end of the cord instead of a bell.

CUTTING GUIDE
• Lower layer, flower 5: 5 patterned petals, each made from a 10.5cm
(4¹/₄in) square of fabric
• Middle layer, flower 3: 7 blue petals, each made from a 7.5cm (3in)
diameter fabric circle
• Felt base: 4cm (1¹/₂in) diameter circle

Basket

Referring to the instructions for flower 5 on page 15, make a six-petal flower, with each petal made from a 20cm (8in) diameter circle of fabric. Finish the back with a 7cm (2¾in) circle of felt. For the centre, gather a 10cm (4in) diameter circle of red spotty fabric around a 5.5cm (2in) diameter circle of card as if you are covering a button. Glue it in the centre of the flower. Pin the cord, ribbon or lace on the back of each petal, 2cm (¾in) from the point to form a basket. Try to space the petals as evenly as possible. Join the ends of the cord under a petal. Sew the cord into place.

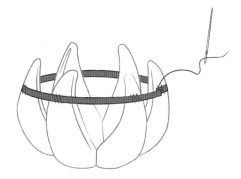

Dashing Dahlias

Dare to be noticed with these eye-catching flowers. The include luxury fabrics you might not ordinarily sew with such as raw silk, silk organza and Chinese satin. You wil only require a little of each, so why not indulge yoursel with these exquisite textiles?

Materials

FOR THE COTTON DAHLIA (1)

- Cotton fabrics: 15 × 40cm (6 × 16in) of mid blue, 15 × 35cm (6 × 13¾in) of patterned blue, 15 × 30cm (6 × 12in) of light blue and 8 × 25cm (3¼ × 10in) of lime green cotton with white spots
- Stuffing for the pearl centre
- Matching mid-blue felt
- Textile adhesive

FOR THE ORGANZA DAHLIA (2)

- Organza: 15 × 40cm (6 × 16in) of dark blue, 15 × 35cm (6 × 13¾in) of mid blue, 15 × 30cm (6 × 12in) of light blue and 8 × 15cm (3¼ × 6in) of green
- Three 8mm (³⁄₈in) iridescent beads
- Matching dark blue felt
- Textile adhesive

FOR THE MULTI-COLOURED DAHLIA (3)

- Mixed fabrics: 18 × 45cm (7 × 17¾in) of patterned blue Chinese satin, 18 × 45cm (7 × 17¾in) of green organza and 8 × 35cm (3¼ × 13¾in) of green silk
- 1.5cm (⁵⁄₈in) blue flower bead
- Matching blue felt
- Textile adhesive

FOR THE SILK DAHLIA (PICTURED ON PAGE 59)

- Raw silk: 15 × 35cm (6 × 13¾in) of dark blue, 15 × 30cm (6 × 12in) of mid blue, 15 × 40cm (6 × 16in) of light blue, 10 × 20cm (4 × 8in) of mid green and a scrap of light-green
- Matching dark blue felt
- Textile adhesive

Cotton dahlia

1 This flower is made in the same way as flower 2 on page 13 but using 6cm (2¼in) diameter circles of fabric for the petals. Start with the lower two layers of petals with 12 mid-blue petals in the bottom layer and 10 patterned blue petals in the middle layer (steps 1–4 on page 13) but do not glue these on to the felt base yet.

2 Make three leaves following the instructions for the petals of flower 3 on page 14, using 6cm (2¼in) diameter circles of fabric.

3 Stick the middle layer of petals on the bottom layer, staggering the petals, and then stick them on to a suitably sized felt base together with the leaves.

4 Make the top layer with eight petals assembled in a spiral as explained in step 5, page 13. Stick it on to the other layers.

5 Make a pearl from a 2cm (³⁄₄in) diameter fabric circle as explained on page 22 and stick it on top to finish your lovely dahlia.

Organza dahlia

This stunning dahlia is made in the same way as the cotton one, but it has three beads in the centre instead of the pearl.

Multi-coloured dahlia

Start this glorious flower in the same way as the cotton dahlia by making two layers of ten petals from fabric circles 7.5cm (3in) in diameter. For the top layer, make flower 3 (see page 14) with petals made from 6cm (2¼in) diameter fabric circles. Stick the three layers on to a felt base. Sew the flower bead into the centre.

Silk dahlia

Make this luxurious flower in the same way as the cotton dahlia, using fabric circles 5cm (2in) in diameter for the bottom two layers of petals and 8.5cm (3¼in) in diameter for the two leaves. Use the small daisy petal maker to make the top layer of blue petals or complete the petals in the same way as the cotton dahlia. For the centre, make a yo-yo from a fabric circle 7cm (2¾in) in diameter (see page 22) or using a small yo-yo maker and stick it in place.

58

Tip

These models are 10–11cm (4–4¼in) in diameter. You can use them as table decorations, attach them to brooches or sew them on to bags.

Floral Wedding

Easy to make and longer lasting than fresh flowers, kanzashi are perfect for special occasions. They look beautiful on personalised place markers and napkin ring or you can even use them to adorn party dresses or wedding-favour bags.

Materials

FOR THE BELT

- Fabrics: 8 × 40cm (3¼ × 16in) of pink poplin, 8 × 40cm (3¼ × 16in) of red poplin and 8 × 45cm (3¼ × 17¾in) of pink print cotton plus 20 × 70cm (8 × 27½in) of white poplin for the belt
- 1cm (½in) porcelain flower
- 1.3m (51in) of silver piping
- 1.25m (49in) of silver cord
- 5cm (2in) of white ribbon 1cm (³⁄₈in) wide
- White felt for the base
- Stuffing for the yo-yos
- Textile adhesive

Belt

Sizing These measurements are for a size 38 inch waist. For other sizes you can easily adapt the length of the band and change the length of the piping to match. The fabric strip should be the size of your waist plus 2cm (³⁄₄in).

The flower Make the two layers of the flower following the instructions in the cutting guide. Stick the top layer on the bottom layer and then stick the flower to the felt base. Stick the porcelain flower into the centre. Fold over 1cm (³⁄₈in) at each end of the ribbon and sew it to the felt base to make a concealed loop as shown.

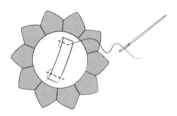

CUTTING GUIDE FOR THE FLOWER

- Bottom layer: 10 petals made with the large gathered-petal flower maker, alternating plain and patterned fabric
- Top layer: 6 petals made using the small round petal maker
- Felt base: 6.5cm (2½in) diameter circle

Making the belt Cut the fabric in half lengthways. Trim the short ends of each strip into a point. You can make a pattern first to ensure the points are exactly the same. Using a zip foot on your machine, sew the piping along the two long sides of one of the strips. Cut the cord in half. Pin a piece at each end of the piped strip to make ties, as shown. Pin the two strips together, right sides together. Sew all round, as close to the piping as possible and sewing through the cord, leaving an opening in the middle. Turn right side out. Sew up the opening using small stitches.

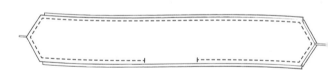

Finishing the ties Make a yo-yo using a circle of fabric around 5cm (2in) in diameter, without cutting the thread (see page 22). Fill with stuffing and pull tight around the end of one cord tie. Sew into place and knot before cutting the thread. Repeat on the other tie.

Wearing the belt Put the belt around your waist so the ends meet at the back, cross the ties behind your back and round to the front, slide them through the flower loop at the front, cross them over again and then knot.

Materials

FOR THE WEDDING-FAVOUR BAGS
• Fabrics: 10 × 50cm (4 × 20in) of white poplin and 18 × 18cm
(3¼ × 3¼in) of red poplin
• 75cm (30in) printed pink bias binding
• Pink pearl cotton embroidery thread
• Two 5mm (¼in) pink beads
• White felt circle around 6cm (2¼in) in diameter
• Textile adhesive

FOR THE PLACE-MARKERS
• Fabrics: 10 × 20cm (4 × 8in) of white poplin and a scrap of printed
pink fabric
• 30cm (12in) silver bias binding
• 2cm (¾in) white flower with a hole in the centre
• 8cm (3¼in) square of thin white card for the name
• Stuffing for the pearl
• White felt for backing
• Textile adhesive

FOR THE NAPKIN RING
• Fabrics: 15 × 40cm (6 × 16in) of white poplin, 15 × 40cm (6 × 16in) of
silver lamé fabric, 8 × 30cm (3¼ × 12in) of pink poplin and 10 × 20cm
(4 × 8in) of pink patterned fabric
• 4mm (¼in) white metal shank button
• 15cm (6in) of silver ribbon, 2cm (¾in) wide
• 6cm (2¼in) circle of felt for backing
• Textile adhesive

Wedding-favour flower

Open up the bias binding so that there is only a central fold. Iron if
necessary. Following the instructions on page 18 create flower 9 with
petals each made from a 10cm (4in) diameter fabric circle. Stick it on to
the white felt base. On the back, fix the bias binding to each petal using a
dab of adhesive. Following the instructions on page 22, make a yo-yo
with a finished diameter of 6cm (2¼in), gathered with pearl cotton: use a
yo-yo maker or make it from a circle of fabric, 16cm (6¼in) in diameter
that you will fold back by 2cm (¾in) all round. Stick the yo-yo into place.
Trim the pearl thread to a good length then thread a bead on at each end
and knot to secure.

Place-marker

Assemble the two petals as for the wedding-favour flower. Neaten the
centre with a pearl made from a circle of fabric 2cm (¾in) in diameter
and a flower-shaped bead. See page 22 for how to make the pearl. Cut a
small circle of felt for the backing. Write the name on the card and stick
on the petals.

Napkin ring

Following the instructions on page 19 for flower 11 and referring to the
cutting guide below, make the lower ring of petals. Refer to the
photograph opposite for colour placement during assembly. Stick the felt
to the back of the flower. Make the upper ring of petals following the
instructions for flower 15 on page 20 and using the very small daisy
petal maker. Stick the small flower on to the big one. Sew the button into
the middle. Now sew the ends of the silver ribbon together with a few
stitches to make a ring. Stick this to the back of the flower.

CUTTING GUIDE
• Lower layer, flower 11: 6 white petals lined in silver and 6 silver petals
lined in white each from a 5cm (2in) square; 4 pink single-layer petals,
each from a 6cm (2¼in) square; 2 patterned pink single-layer petals,
each from a 7.5cm (3in) square
• Upper layer: 10 petals made using the very small daisy petal maker
• Felt base: 6cm (2¼in) in diameter

Forever Autumn

Made with the autumnal colours of orange, green and grey, this pretty collection of jewellery will warm your heart as the cold days approach – and throughout the rest of the year. Use the colours shown or pick your ow to match a favourite outfit.

Materials

FOR THE NECKLACE

• Fabrics: 30 × 60cm (12 × 23½in) of orange cotton sateen, 20 × 20cm (8 × 8in) of green taffeta and 15 × 30cm (6 × 12in) of grey printed cotton

• Two 5mm (¼in) pearly beads

• Stuffing for the pearls

• Findings: two ribbon crimps (ends), 1cm (⅜in) wide; two 5mm (¼in) jump rings and a hook clasp

• 90cm (35½in) of woven ribbon, 1cm (⅜in) wide

• 6.5cm (2½in) circle of orange felt

• Flat-nosed jewellery pliers

• Textile adhesive

Necklace

Large flower Following steps 1–2 for flower 1 on page 12 and using the dimensions in the cutting guide below, make the first petal. Make a leaf as for flower 11 on page 19 but using the dimensions in the cutting guide below and without using a double layer of fabric. Thread the leaf on to your first petal thread. Continue making and threading on the ten petals and leaves alternately. Finish off as for flower 1. Stick the flower on to the felt base. Make the top layer of petals following the instructions on page 17 for flower 7 but using the fabric dimensions in the cutting guide below; stick it on top of the bottom layer. Make a pearl (see page 22) using a 3cm (1¼in) circle of fabric, ensuring that any pattern is centred. Sew it into the centre of the flower.

CUTTING GUIDE FOR THE LARGE FLOWER

• Bottom layer, flower 1: 5 orange petals, each made from a 7.5cm (3in) diameter fabric circle; flower 11 (single layer) for the leaves with 5 green petals, each made from a 5cm (2in) fabric square

• Top layer, flower 7: 7 orange petals, each made from a 5cm (2in) fabric square

• Felt base: 6.5cm (2½in) diameter circle

Smaller flowers Make the medium-sized grey flower following the instructions for flower 1 on page 12 using 5cm (2in) fabric circles for the petals. Make the small orange flower in the same way but with 3cm (1¼in) circles for the petals. For the double flower, gather the petals, putting the smaller petals on top of the larger ones. You don't need a fel base for the middle-sized flowers because they will be sewn directly on to the ribbon. Sew a pearly bead or a taffeta pearl into the centre of each flower. See page 22 to make a pearl.

Assembling the necklace Cut the ribbon in half. Put the two lengths side by side, right sides facing up. Position the flowers where you want them on the ribbons and stitch them on. Trim the ribbons to size if necessary. Insert the ends, one on top of the other, into the ribbon crimps. Stick into place and crimp closed with the jewellery pliers. Connect the clasp to the clamps using jump rings to finish.

Tip
You can use the orchid petal and round petal makers to make the flowers for the necklace.

Materials

For the hair grip

- Fabrics: 8 × 35cm (3¼ × 13¾in) of orange cotton sateen, 8 × 35cm (3¼ × 13¾in) of grey printed cotton and 8 × 8cm (3¼ × 3¼in) of green taffeta
- 2cm (¾in) yellow flower with a hole in the centre
- 8mm (⅜in) pearly bead
- Hair grip, about 10cm (4in) long
- 3cm (1¼in) diameter circle of orange felt for backing
- Textile adhesive

For the brooch

- Fabrics: 15 × 45cm (6 × 18in) of orange cotton sateen, 15 × 20cm (6 × 8in) of grey print cotton and 8 × 20cm (3¼ × 8in) of green taffeta (for the leaves)
- 1cm (⅜in) porcelain flower
- 4cm (1½in) diameter circle of orange felt for backing
- Brooch blank (optional)
- Textile adhesive

Hair grip

The flower is made like flower 1 (see page 12), but by putting a patterned fabric circle, 5cm (2in) in diameter and folded in half, on top of a plain fabric circle, 6cm (2¼in) in diameter and folded in half. Make the leaf as a flower 3 petal, using a fabric circle 6cm (2¼in) in diameter (see page 14). Stick the flower on to the felt base, inserting the leaf between the base and the flower. Thread a needle on to strong thread. Bring it up from the base of the flower, thread on the yellow flower, then the bead and then go back through the yellow flower and your fabric flower. Repeat a few times. Sew the whole thing to the hair grip, passing the needle through the felt base.

Brooch

Make the two layers of this pretty flower following the instructions for flower 7 on page 17: the bottom flower has twelve petals, each made from a 6.5cm (2½in) fabric square, while the top layer has ten petals, each made from a 4.5cm (1¾in) fabric square. Make the three leaves separately, following the instructions for flower 3 on page 14, using 6cm (2¼in) fabric circles. Stick the layers together, staggering the petals. Stick the whole thing on to the felt base. Glue the porcelain flower into the centre to finish. If desired, glue the flower to a brooch blank or pin or stitch it to a garment or accessory.

Tip
You can make this flower using the large and small round petal makers. The leaves should be made as in the instructions above.

Plum Blossom

Materials

FOR THE PENDANT NECKLACE

• Fabrics: 10 × 10cm (4 × 4in) of pink cotton sateen and 5 × 5cm (2 × 2in) of red cotton sateen
• 5mm (¼in) pearly pink bead
• Black jewellery findings: 35–40cm (14–16in) of chain, four 5mm (¼in) jump rings and a lobster clasp
• 1cm (³⁄₈in) diameter circle of pink or red felt for the backing
• Textile adhesive

FOR THE EARRINGS

• Fabrics: 10 × 10cm (4 × 4in) of pink cotton sateen and 10 × 10cm (4 × 4in) of red cotton sateen
• Two 3mm (¹⁄₈in) black beads and two 5mm (¼in) pearly pink beads
• Black jewellery findings: two 3cm (1¼in) lengths of chain, eight 3mm (¹⁄₈in) jump rings, two earring mounts and two headpins
• 1cm (³⁄₈in) diameter circle of matching felt for the backing
• Round-nosed jewellery pliers
• Textile adhesive

Pendant necklace

Following the instructions on page 12 for flower 1, make a flower with four pink petals and one red one, using 3cm (1¼in) diameter circles of fabric. Sew the bead into the centre. Stick the circle of felt on to the back. Sew a jump ring to the edge of the felt, as shown. Attach the clasp to one end of the chain using a jump ring. Attach another jump ring to the other end. Fit the remaining jump ring on to the chain and use it to hang the pendant.

Tip

The flowers for the pendant and earrings are interchangeable. If you prefer the pointed petals of the earring flowers, make one of these for your pendant too.

Materials

FOR THE BROOCH
• Fabrics: 15 × 20cm (6 × 8in) of Japanese-style fabric, 10 × 10cm (4 × 4in) of red cotton sateen and 5 × 5cm (2 × 2in) of pink cotton sateen
• 5mm (¼in) pearly pink bead
• 60cm (23½in) of black suede thong
• Strong black thread
• 3cm (1¼in) diameter circle of pink felt for backing
• Brooch mount, about 3.5cm (1½in) long

Earrings

Flowers Following the instructions on page 14 for flower 3, make a flower with six petals, using 3cm (1¼in) diameter fabric circles and alternating the colours. Sew a black pearl in the centre. Stick the circle of felt on to the back. Sew two jump rings opposite each other on the edge of the felt as in the illustration below. Repeat to make a second flower.

Assembly Slip a pink bead on to a headpin then cut and bend the end of the wire to make a loop (see page 24). Attach it to one end of a chain using a jump ring. Attach the chain to one of the jump rings on the back of each flower using another jump ring. Slide the earring mount into the remaining jump ring on the back of each flower.

Brooch

Flower Following the instructions on page 12 for flower 1, and using 6cm (2¼in) diameter circles of the Japanese-style fabric, create the bottom ring of petals. Make the top petals in the same way but using 3cm (1¼in) diameter circles: here one pink petal was used and four red ones but you can mix and match as you like. Stick the layers together, staggering the petals. Sew the bead into the centre but do not add the felt backing yet.

Tails Cut 25cm (10in) of black thong and fold so one end is shorter than the other. Knot securely with black thread, as shown. Make two loops in a similar fashion with the remaining piece of thong. Place the single loop centrally over the double loop and tie together with thread.

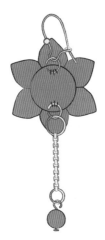

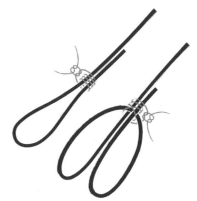

Assembly Stick the flower on to the felt base, inserting the looped thongs between the base and the flower. Sew on to the brooch mount, positioning it slightly above the centre.

Tip
You will find it easier to make very small flowers like these if you use lightweight fabrics.

Crafter's Delight

This useful bag is based on circles of fabric, like a huge yo-yo, so it is easy to make. It opens wide so you can easily find all your bits and pieces. You can also make a matching pincushion and even some jewellery pieces.

Materials

FOR THE CRAFT BAG

- Fabrics: 80 × 80cm (31^1/$_2$ × 31^1/$_2$in) of flower-print cotton, 80 × 80cm (31^1/$_2$ × 31^1/$_2$in) of thick red satin for lining, 80 × 80cm (31^1/$_2$ × 31^1/$_2$in) of iron-on interfacing, 50 × 70cm (20 × 27^1/$_2$in) of black upholstery velour, 50 × 50cm (20 × 20in) of starry black cotton and 12 × 12cm (4^3/$_4$ × 4^3/$_4$in) of polka-dot fabric
- 1.2m (48in) of black starry bias binding
- 16cm (6^1/$_4$in) of matching rouleau cord or cotton cord for a button loop
- 1.1m (43^1/$_2$in) of 5mm (^{1}/$_4$in) dark grey cord
- Stuffing for the pumpkin
- 8mm (^{3}/$_8$in) ornamental button
- String and an erasable fabric marker for drawing the circles

FOR THE PINCUSHION

- 20 × 20cm (8 × 8in) of flower-print cotton
- Red embroidery cotton
- 5mm (^{1}/$_4$in) flower bead
- 1.5cm (^{5}/$_8$in) two-hole red button, ideally flower-shaped
- Stuffing

Craft bag

1 Fuse the interfacing to the wrong side of the flower-print fabric. Using an erasable fabric marker tied to a length of string as a compass, draw a 75cm (29^1/$_2$in) diameter circle (so the string length is 37.5cm or 14^3/$_4$in), on the flower-print cotton and on the red satin. Draw a circle 40cm (16in) in diameter (so the string length is 20cm or 8in) on the black velour and the black star-printed cotton. To make things easier, you can fold the fabrics in half and just draw semi-circles. Cut out.

2 Sew the smaller circles together with right sides facing, leaving an 8cm (3^1/$_4$in) opening, as shown. Turn right side out. Sew up the opening and topstitch all round, just inside the edge.

3 Pin this circle centrally on the big flower-print circle, black velour side up. Use an erasable fabric marker to draw a circle, 16cm (6^1/$_4$in) in diameter, centrally on the smaller circle and topstitch along the line. To make the pockets, draw eight lines dividing the circle into equal segments on the small circle; topstitch along the lines as shown.

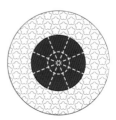

4 Sew the folded bias binding along the long edges to keep it closed like a ribbon. Cut twelve 10cm (4in) pieces. Fold each one in half to make a loop and pin the loops at regular intervals inside the edge of the large circle to form the tabs for the cord handles. Fold the short length of cord for the button loop in half and pin it to the fabric in the same way as the binding loops, placing it centrally between two loops, as shown.

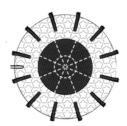

Tip

Instead of using bias binding for the cord tabs, which you will need to stitch closed, you can use herringbone tape. This comes in a number of different colours and is very strong.

5 Pin the red lining on top of your main piece, with right sides facing. Sew together all round, leaving an opening of 10cm (4in) to turn through. Turn right side out. Sew up the opening and topstitch all round, just inside the edge.

6 Thread the cord through the tabs and sew the ends together. Cut two rectangles of velour 10 × 20cm (4 × 8in) for the handles. Fold the short ends to the wrong side by 1cm (³/₈in) and topstitch. Fold the long sides over to the wrong side, as shown to make the handles. Fold a handle around the cord (over its join) and sew the two long edges together. Adjust so the seam runs down the centre underside of the handle rather than the edge and then sew with a few hand stitches across the short ends again to ensure the handle remains fixed on the cord. Repeat for the second handle, making sure it is at exactly the same height.

7 Make a pumpkin using a circle of fabric around 10cm (4in) in diameter (see page 22). After you have made the segments, sew the ornamental button into the middle, stitching right through the pumpkin. Sew it into place, opposite the loop.

Pincushion

Following the instructions on page 22, make the pincushion as a pumpkin from a circle of fabric with a diameter of around 18cm (7in), or using a very large yo-yo maker. Once you have made the segments, thread a needle with strong thread. Take it up from the bottom, through one hole of the button, through the flower bead, back through the second hole in the button and then through the pumpkin. Repeat a few times then knot off neatly on the bottom.

Tip
Sew or stick a small felt circle under the pincushion to neaten it.

Materials

FOR THE CHOKER

- Fabrics: 20 × 20cm (8 × 8in) of flower print cotton and 10 × 20cm (4 × 8in) of black star-patterned cotton
- 80cm (31½in) of rouleau cord (here made from the star-print fabric)
- Embroidery thread in white and red
- Three 1cm (³/₈in) flowers beads, one red and two black
- Two large seed beads (or more if desired)
- Stuffing for the pumpkins and pearls

FOR THE BRACELET

- 30 × 40cm (12 × 16in) of red cotton sateen
- Scrap of flower-print cotton
- 2cm (³/₄in) diameter red felt circle
- 18cm (7in) of rouleau cord (here made from the star-print fabric)
- One seed bead
- Findings: two crimp ends to fit your cord, two 6mm (¼in) jump rings and a lobster clasp
- Flat-nosed jewellery pliers
- Stuffing for the pearl
- Multi-purpose glue

Crafter's choker

Pumpkins Referring to the instructions on page 22 and the photograph opposite for your fabric choices, make three pumpkins from circles of fabric with a diameter of around 9cm (3½in), or using a large yo-yo maker. If the fabric pattern is a repeating one, make sure it is centred in the same place for each pumpkin. Once you have made the segments, you can embroider short straight stitches radiating out from the centre for added decoration. Sew on the flower beads.

Pearls Referring to the instructions on page 22, make six pearls from circles of fabric 4cm (1½in) in diameter, ensuring that any pattern is centred. Sew a seed bead centrally on two of them.

Assembly Starting from the centre, sew the fabric pumpkins and pearls on to the rouleau cord, leaving a gap of around 5mm (¼in) between each one. Refer to the photograph opposite for placement. Trim the ends of the cord if necessary for a good fit: this necklace should be worn fairly tightly around the neck so the decorations do not tip forwards. You can also wear it in your hair as a hair band. For a longer necklace, position the fabric cord higher up on the pumpkins.

Bracelet

Flower Make a nine-petal red flower using a very small daisy petal flower maker or another flower of your choice. Stick it on to the felt base. Make a pearl from a 4cm (1½in) diameter circle of flowery fabric, ensuring that the pattern is centred (see page 22). Sew the fabric pearl into the centre of the flower, holding it in place with a seed bead, as shown in the photograph.

Assembly Sew the flower into the centre of the fabric cord. Check the cord length (see the tip) then insert one end of the cord into a crimp end. Dab in a bit of glue, and crimp closed using the pliers. Repeat at the other end. Attach the clasp parts to each crimp end using the jump rings.

Tip

Before adding the crimp ends to the cord for the bracelet, check that the cord fits your wrist bearing in mind the added length of the jump rings and clasp.

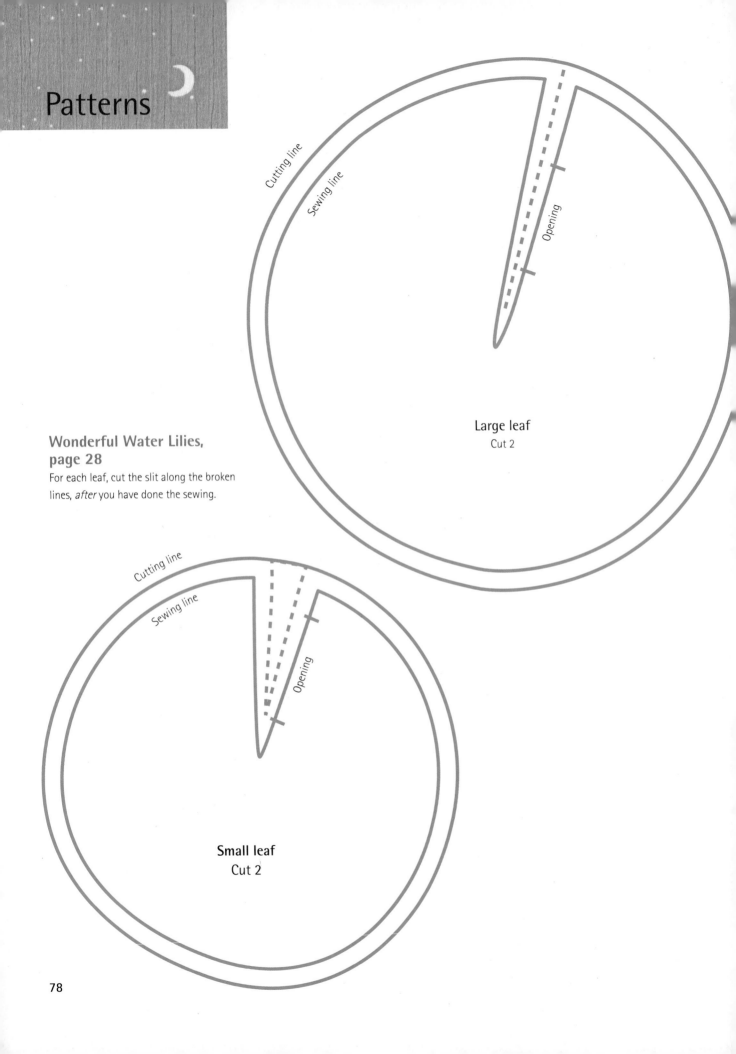

Patterns

Large leaf
Cut 2

Cutting line

Sewing line

Opening

**Wonderful Water Lilies,
page 28**
For each leaf, cut the slit along the broken lines, *after* you have done the sewing.

Cutting line

Sewing line

Opening

Small leaf
Cut 2

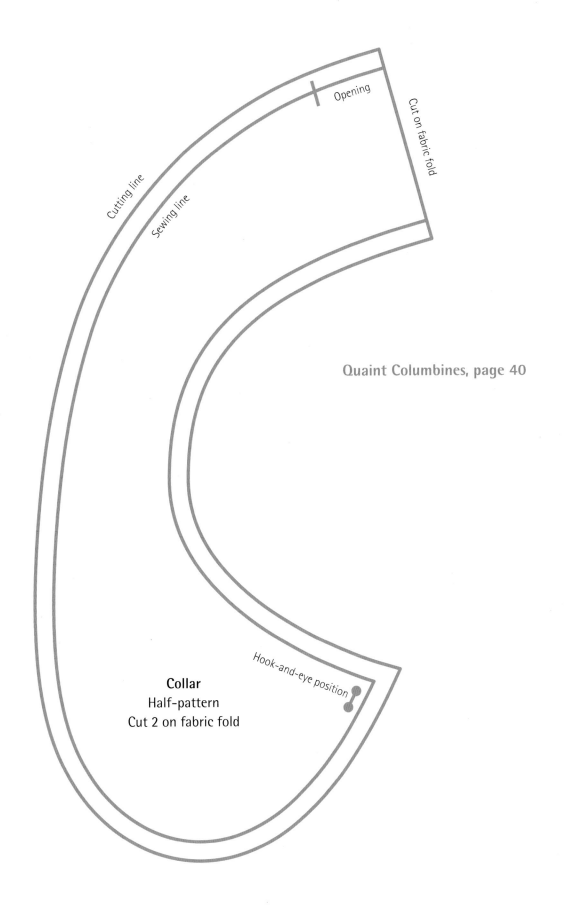

Opening

Cutting line

Sewing line

Cut on fabric fold

Quaint Columbines, page 40

Hook-and-eye position

Collar
Half-pattern
Cut 2 on fabric fold